The Connection of TILII Dzi

-Book 3-

Herbs, Oils, and Incenses

by Tilii Bolin

The Connection of TILII Dzi – Book 3 – Herbs, Oils, and
Incenses

Copyright © 2019 by Tilii Bolin

Tilii Bolin

P.O. Box 252

Crab Orchard, TN 37723

Library of Congress Cataloging-inPublicationData

Type of Work: Text

Registration Number / Date: Txu 2-164-492/ 2019-11-05

The Connection of TILII Dzi

-Book 3-

Herbs, Oils, and Incenses

- FORWARD -

The Dzi bead is the most mystical item found in the world. With the recent discovery of Dzi in the Western World, the gates of knowledge have now been opened.

The bead itself is made of Agate, and has an unexplained "eye". The eye is known to have extraordinary powers among the monks of Tibet. The pattern created upon the Dzi holds a specific intent. These beads are described in detail for the first time in the English language in "The Complete Book of Dzi Beads".

With so many theories and rumors circulating, the true order of the correlating factors of the Dzi had been long ago lost. They are now listed within the Tilii books. These factors are composed of gemstones, oils derived from herbs, incense scents, etc, with the alike meaning of each Dzi bead variety.

Combined in an algebraic algorithm that flows harmoniously within the boundaries of the natural constructs of the human reality, the Key of Tilii Dzi provides the reader with the "key" to alignment according to the Doctrine of Signatures.

The Doctrine of Signatures is the vibrational and frequency correlation law book and character trait map of many alike things. Such as a Rose, the color red, the gemstone Rose Quartz, the frequency 528hz, they all correlate to the emotion of love. While EVERYTHING is scientifically proven to be composed of energy, tapping into "grid" is made possible by this grand alignment of alike energies along with focused intent. If you believe, so shall it become. Let the reader understand.

When worn, the subconscious is consistently aware of the necklace and therefore is constantly also aware of its intent. By way of the Universal Laws, which do not change or vary, what you put out, is what you receive. This is the Law of

Attraction.

The Law of Attraction is the belief that by focusing on positive or negative thoughts, people can bring positive or negative experiences into their life.

The Connection of Tilii Dzi – Book 3 – Herbs, Oils, and Incenses continues the journey into manifestation via alignment of alike signatures to "connect to the grid" aka "the matrix". In this book you will find the correlating herbs, oils, and incenses to heighten connection with the meaning of the Dzi bead, as well as the gemstones to further amplify its specific intent. This is the algebraic frequency equation for each necklace for optimal power.

- TABLE OF CONTENTS -

Herbs Utilized and Their Signatures

Oil Recipes

Incenses Utilized and Their Signatures

DZI Bead Connection Correlation

Prayers (Special Gift From Me to You)

Conclusion

- HERBS UTILIZED AND THEIR SIGNATURES -

ACACIA - protection, psychic and spiritual enhancement, money, platonic love, and friendship

AGRIMONY – overcoming fear and inner blockages; dispelling negative emotions. Also used for reversing spells

ALFALFA LEAF – money, prosperity, anti-hunger

ALLSPICE – money, luck, healing, obtaining treasure, provides added determination and energy

ALTHEA - protection, calm an angry person, and aid psychic powers

ALUM – removes the evil eye

AMBER GUM - protection from harm, outside influences, and psychic attacks, mental clarity and focus, transforming negative energy to positive energy

ANGELICA – remove curses, hexes, or spells

ANISE SEED – helps ward off the evil eye, find happiness, and stimulate psychic ability

ARROWROOT – purification and healing

ASAFOETIDA – protection and banishing negativity

ASTER – love

BAT NUTS – repels, wards off

BALSAM FIR – strength and breaking up negativity; Insight, progress against goals, and bringing about change

BARBERRY – Cleansing, sorcery, atonement, freeing oneself from the power or control of another.

BASIL – love, exorcism, wealth, sympathy, and protection. Dispels confusion, fears and weakness, drives off hostile spirits

BAT PETALS – success, money, luck

BAY LEAF - protection, good fortune, success, purification, strength, healing and psychic powers

BEARBERRY – psychic abilities

BERGAMOT – money, prosperity, protection

from evil and illness, improving memory, stopping interference, and promoting restful sleep

BILBERRY FRUIT – protection

BILBERRY LEAF – protection, burn for material desires

BLACK SNAKE ROOT – protection

BLACK COHOSH – love, courage, protection and potency

BLADDERWACK – protection, sea spells, wind spells, money, psychic powers, and attracting customers

BLESSED THISTLE – purification, protection against negativity and evil, hex breaking

BLOODROOT – love, protection, and

purification

BLUE COHOSH - empowerment, purification, money drawing, love breaking, and driving away evil

BLUE VERVAIN – divination, cleansing

BONESET – protection, exorcism and warding off evil spirits

BORAGE – courage, cheerfulness

BUCKTHORN BARK - luck generator in legal matters and for winning in court

BURDOCK ROOT – cleansing and protection

BUTTERCUP - restore your inner child and bring calmness, joy and sweetness into your life

CALAMUS ROOT – luck, money, healing, and protection

CALENDULA – protection, legal matters, and psychic/spiritual powers

CALEA ZACATECHICHI – relaxation and intense dreams

CAMPHOR - dreams, psychic awareness, and divination; Adds strength to any mixture; used for purification and to increase personal influence & persuasiveness

CARAWAY SEED – health, love, protection, mental powers, memory, passion, and anti-theft

CASCARA SAGRADA – legal matters, money spells and protection against hexes

CATNIP – love, luck, and attraction

CATS CLAW – vision quests, shamanic journeys, and money drawing

CAYENNE PEPPER – dealing with separations or divorce; cleansing & purification; repels negativity

CEDAR – confidence, strength, power, money, protection, healing and purification

CELERY FLAKES – mental powers, psychic powers, lust, fertility, and male potency

CELERY SEED – mental and psychic powers, concentration

CHAMOMILE – love, healing, and reducing stress

CHAPARREL – protection and overcoming

CHICKWEED – fidelity and love

CHICORY ROOT – frigidity, favors, removing obstacles, and invisibility. Promotes a positive outlook and improves sense of humor

CHILI PEPPER – fidelity, love, and hex breaking

CINNAMON – spirituality, success, healing, protection, power, love, luck, strength, and prosperity

CINQUEFOIL - stimulates memory, eloquence, and self confidence

CLEAVER – healing, sticking ability

CLOVER - fidelity, protection, money, love, and success

CLOVES – protection, banishing hostile/negative forces, and gaining what is sought

CLUB MOSS – protection and power, purification

COLTSFOOT – wealth, prosperity, and love

COMFREY – money, safety during travel

COPAL ORO – purification and love

CORRANDER SEED – love, health, immortality, and protection

CORNSILK – love

COUCHGRASS – defense, returning to sender

CRAMP BARK – protection, female energy,

psychic ability

CRUEL MAN OF THE WOODS – adds power and defeats evil

CUMIN – fidelity, protection, and exorcism

DAMINANA – sex, love, and luck

DANDELION LEAF – summoning spirits, healing, purification and defeating negativity

DANDELION ROOT - divination, wishes and calling spirits

DEER TONGUE - divination, wishes and calling spirits

DEVILS CLAW – protection and dispelling unwanted company

DEVILS SHOWSTRING – protection, luck, attracting a new raise or job, giving control over opposite sex, and invisibility

DILL SEED – protection, money, lust, and luck

DITTANY OF CRETE - astral projection, spirit evocation and manifestation

DRAGONS BLOOD – protection, energy, and purification

ECHINACEA – adds powerful strength, money drawing

EGGSHELL – repels negative and protection

ELDERBERRY – healing, blessing, banishing, and cleansing

ELDER FLOWERS – sleep, releasing

enchantments, protection against negativity, wisdom, house blessing and business blessing

ELECAMPANE - banishing and to dispel angry or violent vibrations

EUCALYPTUS LEAF - Attracts healing vibrations, great for protection and healing, purification

EYEBRIGHT – increase psychic ability, improve memory, encourage rationality and increase positive outlook

FAVA BEANS - love, wishes and courage, gain prosperity & courage, grants luck and protects from disease and/or to attract love, promotes the accomplishment of goals

FENNEL SEED – imparts strength, vitality, sexual virility; prevents curses, possession and negative problems

FENUGREEK SEED – money drawing and fertility magick

FEVERFEW – healing, relaxation, love, and banishing

FIVE FINGER GRASS – repels evil, luck

FLAX SEED – money and protection

FRANKINCENSE – successful ventures, cleansing, purification, protection, consecration, and meditation

GALANGAL – winning in court, doubling money, hex breaking and sex magick

GARLIC – healing, protection, exorcism, repulsion of vampires, and purification of spaces and objects . Hecate

GINGER – draws adventure and new experiences. Promotes sensuality, sexuality, personal confidence, prosperity, and success

GINKO – aphrodisiac, associated with fertility, healing

GINSENG - love, beauty, protection, healing and lust

GOLDEN ROD – peace, love, money, and prosperity

GOLDENSEAL ROOT – attraction, warding off evil, luck, healing

GOTU KOLA – aphrodisiac, longevity, breaks and returns

GRAVEL ROOT – job, money, and luck

GUINEA PEPPER – luck, job, power

GUM ARABIC – protection, psychic and spiritual enhancement, money, platonic love, and friendship

HIBISCUS – attracting love and lust, divination, and dreams

HIGH JOHN ROOT – strength, confidence, conquering any situation, obtaining success, winning at gambling, luck, money, love, health, and protection

HOREHOUND – protective; helps with mental clarity during ritual; stimulates creativity/inspiration; balances personal energies

HORSE CHESTNUT – money and healing

HYSSOP – purification, lightens vibrations and promotes spiritual opening, cleansing and purification. protect property against burglars and trespassers

JASMINE – prophecy, attraction, moon magick, and charges crystals

JEZEBEL – money and achievement

JUNIPER – banishes all things injurious to good health; attracts good, healthy energies and love

KAVA KAVA – aphrodisiac, invites good, visions

KELP – healing and attraction

LAVENDER – love, protection, healing, sleep, purification, and peace, promotes healing from depression

LEMON BALM - Love, success, healing, and psychic/spiritual development

LEMONGRASS – warding off and forgiving

LEMON PEEL – cleansing, spiritual opening, purification, and removal of blockages

LEMON VERBENA – breaking bad habits, purify body

LICORICE ROOT – love, lust, and fidelity

LIFE EVERLASTING – health and longevity

LOBELIA – attracting love and preventing storms

LOVAGE ROOT – prophetic dreams, energy, and purification

MANDRAKE ROOT – protection, prosperity, fertility, and exorcising evil

MARJORAM LEAF – cleansing, purification, and dispelling negativity

MARSHMELLOW LEAF - protection and psychic powers

MARSHMELLOW ROOT – protection, fertility, sexual, and clairvoyance

MASTER OF THE WOODS – protection, commanding

MAYAPPLE ROOT – protection, to hide emotions

MEADOWSWEET – protection, love, and harmony

MINT – promotes energy, communication and vitality, draws customers to a business

MISTLETOE – fertility, creativity,

prevention of illness/misfortune, and protection

MOTHERWORT –bolstering ego, building confidence, success

MUGWORT – increase lust and fertility, prevent backache and cure disease and madness

MULLEIN – courage, determination, guards against evil, and divination

MUSK – encourages self-esteem and desirability

MUSTARD SEED – courage, faith, and endurance

MYRRH – spiritual opening, meditation, and healing

NETTLE LEAF – dispelling darkness & fear,

strengthening the will, and aiding in the ability to handle emergencies

NUTMEG – attracting money/prosperity, bringing luck, protection, and breaking hexes

OATS – prosperity

OATSTRAW – money and prosperity

OAT TOPS – purification, wind, divination, and protection

OLIVE LEAF - peace, potency, fertility, healing, protection and lust

ONION - prosperity, stability, endurance, and protection

ORANGE PEEL - love, divination, luck, money and house & business blessing

OREGANO - Joy, strength, vitality, and added energy

ORRIS - bring love, romance, companionship and a loving mate

PALO SANTO – breaks curses and hexes

PAPRIKA - adds energy

PARSLEY – calms and protects the home; Draws prosperity, financial increase, and luck. Restores a sense of well-being

PASSION FLOWER - attracting friendship and prosperity and heightening libido, brings great popularity & attract new friends

PATCHOULI - money & love

PAU D'ARCO – protection, brings vision and wisdom, healing of severe diseases

PENNYROYAL – peace and tranquility

PEPPERMINT – divination, money, protection, purification, healing, and wind

PERIWINKLE – love within marriage, mental powers, and money

PINE – promotes clean breaks, new beginnings, prosperity, success, strength, grounding, and growth; Also used for cleansing, purification, and repelling negativity

PLANTAIN LEAF – protection from evil spirits and snake bites, removing weariness, healing headaches; house & business blessing

POKE ROOT – finding lost objects and

breaking hexes and curses, increases courage

POPPY SEED – pleasure, heightened awareness, love, luck, invisibility

PURPLE DEAD NETTLE - help improve the health of the spirit as well as the body

QUEEN OF THE MEADOW - protection and harmony

RASPBERRY LEAF – healing, protection, love, reduces labor pain

RED CLOVER – fidelity, love, money, protection, and the blessing of domestic animals

RED SANDALWOOD – protection, healing, exorcism, bringing success, and increasing opportunity

RICE – money drawing

ROSE – love and beauty

ROSE HIPS - healing, brings good luck, calls in good spirits

ROSEMARY – protection, healing, and cleansing

RUE - healing, health, mental powers, freedom and protection against the evil eye

SAGE – self purification and dealing with grief and loss, improves mental ability and bring wisdom, healing, promotes spiritual, mental, emotional and physical health and longevity, removes negative energy

SALT PETRE – stops sexual tension

SANDALWOOD – protection, healing, and

exorcism

SAW PALMETTO – healing protection, exorcism, passion and spiritual openings

SENNA – all matters of lust and love, enhances tact and diplomacy

SESAME SEED – money, lust, and passion

SHAVEGRASS – fertility

SHEEP SORREL – healing

SHEPHARDS PURSE – prosperity, protection against bleeding

SKULLCAP – fidelity and money

SLIPPERY ELM BARK – guarding and stops gossip

SOAPWORT – empowers love spells, love, and healing

SOLOMONS SEAL – protection from evil

SPANISH MOSS – protection, opening blockages, and dispelling negativity

SPEARMINT LEAF – healing, love and protection while sleeping

STAR ANISE - increase psychic awareness & abilities

ST. JOHNS WORT – protection, banishing, blessing, and rids of sorrow

STRAWBERRY LEAF – attracts success, good fortune, and favorable circumstances

SULFUR – dispels or prevents a hex on you; destroys an enemy's power over you

SWEETGRASS - Peace, unity, and calling spirits

TARRAGON – healing in abuse situations, compassion

THYME – attracts loyalty, affection, and the good opinion of others

TURMERIC – wards off evil

VALERIAN ROOT – protection, calm, love purification, harmony, and ending guilt

VERVAIN – protection, purification, money, youth, peace, healing, and sleep

WHEAT – fertility and money

WHITE OAK BARK – protection, fertility, removing bad

WHITE SAGE – cleansing, repels bad spirits

WHITE WILLOW BARK - brings blessing and guards against negativity and evil forces

WINTERGREEN - good fortune and luck

WITCH HAZEL – chastity and protection, inspiration

WOOD BOTANY – purification, protection, and the expulsion of evil spirits, nightmares, and despair

WOOD SORREL - health, healing, luck, prophecy

WORMWOOD – remove anger, stop war, inhibit violent acts, and for protection from the evil eye

YARROW – healing, weddings, and divination, draws love, banishes negativity, wards off fear, and promotes courage, confidence, and psychic openings

YELLOW DOCK - fertility, healing and money

YERBA MATE – love, luck, and fidelity

- OIL RECIPES -

PATH CLEARING

3 CINNAMON

9 BAY LEAVES

9 CLOVES

LEMON BALM

SANDALWOOD

FIVE FINGER GRASS

PINE NEEDLES

3 CAMPHOR TABLETS

ALMOND OR OLIVE OIL

WEALTH ATTRACTING

3 LODESTONES

THYME

ROSEMARY

3 CINNAMON

3 CLOVES

DILL SEED

1 QUARTER

1 DIME

1 NICKEL

1 PENNY

DOLLAR OR GREATER

SHREDDED MONEY

OLIVE OIL

GIVE AND TAKE

4 LEAF CLOVER

3 PYRITE

LODESTONES

3 FAVA BEANS (MOJO WISH BEANS)

SWEET GRASS

LEMON VERBENA

LEMON GRASS

SULFUR

DILL SEED

OLIVE OIL

RELEASING

CAYENNE PEPPER

PEPPERMINT

RUE

ROSEMARY

3 PINE NEEDLES

ONYX

OLIVE OIL

ATTENTION

ANGELICA

CEDAR CHIPS

CALAMUS ROOT

LICORICE ROOT

LEMON VERBENA

CATNIP FOR ATTRACTING

DAMIANA FOR SEXUALITY

CORIANDER OR LOW JOHN FOR LAW

OLIVE OIL

ENLIGHTENMENT

3 GARLIC

ROSEMARY

BASIL

BAY

OLIVE OIL

EXPANSION

MYRRH

CINNAMON

GALANGAL

CALAMUS

CASSIA

OLIVE OIL

ASSISTANCE

PARSLEY

SAGE

ROSEMARY

THYME

OLIVE OIL

– <u>INCENSES UTILIZED AND THEIR SIGNATURES</u> -

ALOE VERA - emotional balance, stimulates the brain function, and amplifies thought

AMBER - wisdom and truth-seeking, as well as rituals of love and desire

APPLE - happiness, love and friendship

AYURVEDA - harmony, peace and quietness

CANNABIS - relaxing atmosphere

CHANDAN - purifying

CHERRY - fertility and love-producing

CINNAMON - Stimulation, wealth, prosperity, business success, strength, lust, healing, to attract money, stimulate and strengthen the psychic powers, and to aid in healing. To gain wealth and success

CITRUS - confidence and good luck, extra energy to accomplish goals, joy, good fortune, and prosperity, and happiness in marriage.

CLOVE - pain relief, intellectual stimulation, business success, wealth, prosperity, divination, exorcism, protection, eases fears, improves memory and focus

COCONUT - divination and love

DRAGONS BLOOD - protection, purification, courage, dispel negativity, attract love, enhance psychic awareness

FRANKINCENSE - purification, power, and riches

JASMINE - meditation and psychic sight, encourage prophetic dreams

LAVENDER - refreshing the body, mind, and home environment

LILY - Protection

MAGNOLIA - fidelity

MYRRH -spirituality, meditation, healing and consecration. An ancient incense for protection, healing, purification and spirituality

MUSK - aphrodisiac, prosperity, courage,

creates a sensual atmosphere. For courage and vitality, or to heighten passion

NAG CHAMPA - aid to meditation and may be used as general

OPIUM - seeking knowledge or consulting with spirits

PALO SANTO - medicinal and therapeutic healing

PATCHOULI – attraction, Sex, and money

ROSE - attract and keep true love; Both romantic love and self-love

SAGE - wisdom, clarity and purification

SANDALWOOD - spirituality, healing, protection, astral projection to heal and protect, also for purification

STRAWBERRY - love, luck and friendship

SUPER HIT - reduce the negative and increase the positive

VANILLA - happiness, prosperity, and knowledge-seeking

VIOLET - wisdom, luck, love, protection and healing

- DZI BEAD CONNECTION CORRELATION -

Aristocrat

The Aristocrat Dzi will give you self-confidence, will attract friends, partners, protectors, and advisers to you. It will correct your karma and will slay the demons.

HERBS : AGRIMONY, HIGH JOHN ROOT, BALSAM FIR, BLACK SNAKE ROOT, HORSE CHESTNUT, CALAMUS ROOT, CATNIP, CEDAR, WINTERGREEN

OIL : ASSISTANCE

INCENSE : CITRUS

Aquarius Bottle

The Aquarius Bottle Dzi looks like a heart shaped bottle usually with a cross at the top. This Dzi assists the owner by preventing disease. The Aquarius Bottle Dzi can help the owner to increase their income. It is believed that this Dzi has the power to eradicate sadness and suffering. It is said to attract luck for its possessor, helps to make money, and enables the possessor to become healthier. The Aquarius Bottle Dzi is always a target for Dzi bead collectors, making good Dzis harder to find.

HERBS : ARROWROOT, HOREHOUND, HYSSOP, COLTSFOOT, GARLIC, NETTLE LEAF, CAMPHOR, PURPLE DEAD NETTLE, YARROW

OIL : PATH CLEARING

INCENSE : PALO SANTO

Bat

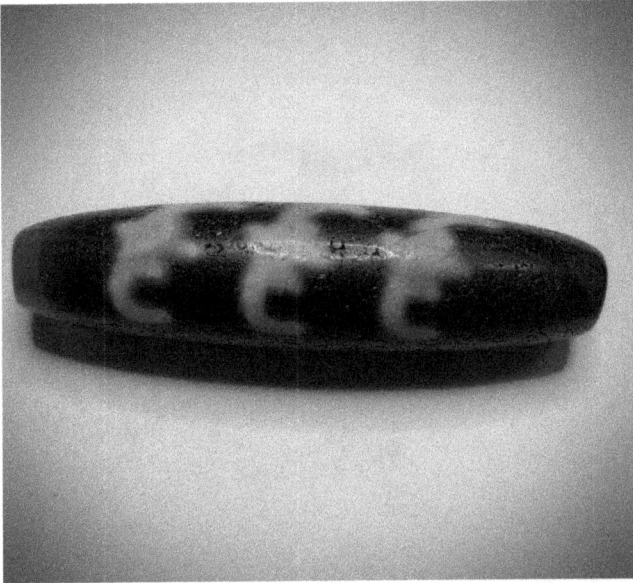

This Dzi can gift to its owner incredible luck and get him into the life full of amazing events and opportunities. If we take into consideration the fact that the bat is also a symbol of wealth, then the bead becomes a powerful tool to acquire wealth and prosperity.

HERBS : YERBA MATE, JASMINE, LIFE EVERLASTING, LANENDER, SKULLCAP, LEMON BALM, CHAPARREL, CASCARA SAGRADA, CATNIP

OIL : PATH CLEARING

INCENSE : PATCHOULI

Bear

The Bear Dzi is a forest embodiment of Tara. It is the image of a bear, who is keeping a gold bar in his paws. It refers to Golden Tara which brings prosperity and protection.

HERBS : CATS CLAW, ANISE SEED, ACACIA, SHEPHERDS PURSE, COLTSFOOT, CRUEL MAN OF THE WOODS, GALANGAL, OATS, NUTMEG

OIL : WEALTH ATTRACTING

INCENSE : VANILLA

Bodhi

The Bohdi Dzi bead establishes good virtues and eliminates misfortune in your life, giving you a generous and lenient heart. This Dzi bead helps to avoid dangers, aids in growth in compassion, as well as wisdom & enlightenment. The Bodhi Dzi establishes good virtues and eliminates life's misfortunes, helping the possessor to avoid dangers.

HERBS : CALENDULA, LAVENDER, CATNIP, SWEETGRASS, DAMIANA, CALEA ZACATECHICHI, CINNAMON, CLOVES, FAVA BEANS

OIL : ASSISTANCE

INCENSE : FRANKINCENSE AND MYRRH

Buddha

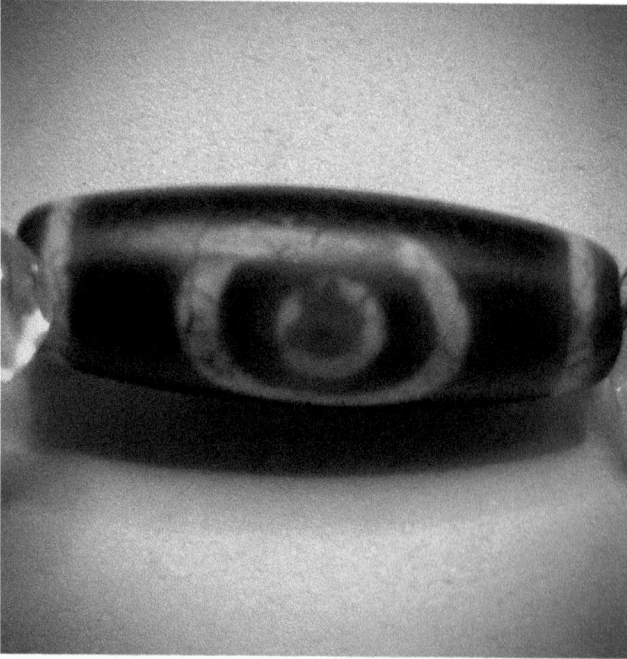

   The Buddha-eyed Dzi is a beacon of light and hope. It is believed the stone gives the person who wears the Dzi special power in realizing his/her dreams. This Dzi is also a necessary component when crafting a Dragon Eye Dzi necklace. It brings life-long happiness.

HERBS : CLOVER, JEZEBEL, MYRRH, ORANGE PEEL, PAU D'ARCO, RASPBERRY LEAF, ALFALFA LEAF, FLAX SEED, GINGER

OIL : ASSISTANCE

INCENSE : JASMINE

Dharma Hat (Padmasambhava – Lotiform)

The Dharma Hat Dzi, also known as The Padmasambhava Dzi has a flattened heart shape with a small hook in it. The Dharma Hat motif on this Dzi bead is a symbol of holy protection. This Dzi bead is a spiritual object or talisman.

HERBS : BAY, BASIL, ROSEMARY, RUE, ALTHEA, ALUM, QUEEN OF THE MEADOW, WORMWOOD, WINTERGREEN

OIL : RELEASING

INCENSE : DRAGONS BLOOD

Dharma Wheel (Dharmacakra)

The Dharma Wheel Dzi, also known as The Dharmacakra Dzi, is one of the most powerful Dzi with the energy of Luck. The symbol applied on it resembles Dharmacakra started by Shakyamuni Buddha when he began his sermon. The Dharma Wheel Dzi will help you to obtain wisdom, to avoid serious mistakes in life, to achieve enlightenment, and to call for help.

HERBS : BAT PETALS, BAY LEAF, CELERY SEED, DILL SEED, FRANKINCENSE, LEMON PEEL, KELP, PARSLEY, PENNYROYAL

OIL : ASSISTANCE

INCENSE : OPIUM

Diamond and Pestle

   The Diamond and Pestle Dzi is one of the healer Dzis. It assists the mind of the healer and will be of most benefit in the hands of a healer, rather than a layman. It has diamonds with pestles in between the diamonds. This Dzi enhances the mind of the healer to assist in finding the recipes that will do the greatest good for the patient. The Diamond and Pestle Dzi is known as a magical instrument to keep ghosts from the human body and to improve health & wisdom.

HERBS : AMBER GUM, CARAWAY SEED, DEVILS SHOESTRING, DRAGONS BLOOD, GOLDENSEAL ROOT, JUNIPER, MAJORAM LEAF, PLANTAIN LEAF, GUINEA PEPPER

OIL : PATH CLEARING

INCENSE : ALOE VERA

Dog

The Dog Dzi offers protection, alertness, bravery, devotion and constancy. This Dzi also encourages you to evaluate the people who have treated you badly and how you are dealing with them. No longer let their existence affect you, because it does nothing for you but make you feel less than, and live in uncertainty.

HERBS : BAY LEAF, BURDOCK ROOT, CEDAR, CHICORY ROOT, CRUEL MAN OF THE WOODS, DEVILS CLAW, LEMON GRASS, MASTER OF THE WOODS, SOLOMONS SEAL

OIL : PATH CLEARING

INCENSE : SAGE

Double Fishes

The Double Fishes Dzi is a very symbolic Dzi which represents abundance and wealth. ... Yu, which means fish, phonetically matches the word for abundance, which might be a coincidence but is very symbolic as well. This Dzi will bring abundance and wealth to its possessor.

HERBS : RED CLOVER, ALLSPICE, BAT PETALS, CALAMUS ROOT, COLTSFOOT, FENUGREEK SEED, GRAVEL ROOT, RICE, SESAME SEED

OIL : WEALTH ATTRACTING

INCENSE : CINNAMON

Dragon

The Dragon Dzi symbolizes protection and it is beheld as the ultimate entity over all other creatures.

HERBS : ROSE HIPS, RUE, SOLOMONS SEAL, STAR ANISE, HIGH JOHN ROOT, BAY LEAF, ALUM, FRANKINCENSE, MYRRH

OIL : ENLIGHTENMENT

INCENSE : FRANKINCENSE

Dragon Eyed

Each Dragon Eyed Dzi is connected to a dragon, and each dragon may be connected to several different Dzi beads. The Dragon Eyed Dzi connects the human owner to the dragon they will master.

HERBS : ROSE HIPS, RUE, SOLOMONS SEAL, STAR ANISE, HIGH JOHN ROOT, BAY LEAF, ALUM, FRANKINCENSE, MYRRH

OIL : ASSISTANCE

INCENSE : FRANKINCENSE

Eagle's Mouth

This Dzi symbolizes a life of comfort and the fulfillment of all wishes. It has the ability to turn adverse situations into auspicious ones.

HERBS : SLIPPERY ELM BARK, STRAWBERRY LEAF, LAVENDER, ROSE, SOAPWORT, JASMINE, JUNIPER, HIBISCUS, POPPY SEED

OIL : ENLIGHTENMENT

INCENSE : AYURVEDA

Garuda Healing (Mythical Bird)

The Garuda Dzi enhances fame and recognition, luck, dispels bad luck, clears confusion, protects from danger, banishes evil spirits, and alleviates illness. This Dzi is best for people seeking high visibility from those surrounding them. It carries great power and strength and is used to overthrow any enemy or evil.

HERBS : LEMON PEEL, ORANGE PEEL, JEZEBEL, NETTLE LEAF, OATSTRAW, ALLSPICE, BARBERRY, BLUE COHOSH, BILBERRY FRUIT

OIL : RELEASING

INCENSE : CITRUS

Guru Rinpoche's Ritual Paraphernalia Motif / Scepter Motif

The implement of esoteric. Subduing demons and expelling evil obstructions. Greatly improves the concentration of meditation, reaching the ultimate beyond emotion or thinking.

A variation, The Guru Rinpoche's Ritual Scepter Motif is believed to have the power to subdue demons and evil obstructions, as well as helping to improve concentration when meditating, thus helping to bring enlightenment.

HERBS : BLESSED THISTLE, BLUE COHOSH, BONESET, CAYENNE PEPPER, COUCHGRASS, FIVE FINGER GRASS, SANDALWOOD, SAW PALMETTO, AMBER GUM

OIL : PATH CLEARING

INCENSE : SUPER HIT

Heaven & Earth

The Heaven and Earth Dzi creates flawlessness in all areas of one's life. It is believed that the Heaven and Earth Dzi will assist its possessor in achieving balance and harmony in their life. It also aids in clearing any obstacles which may cause harm to its owner. Wealth and good health will also be bestowed on its possessor.

Double Heaven and Earth gives maximal advancement.

HERBS : ALLSPICE, ANGELICA, BAY, CALENDULA, CINNAMON, CLOVE, COMFREY, GINGER, DILL, MINT, CHAMOMILE, NUTMEG, SAGE, ROSEMARY

OIL : EXPANSION

INCENSE : FRANKINCENSE

Heart

Our life and power are in the heart. This Dzi aids us in restoring the connection with this power, to find ourselves, and to obtain control over the potential of the body, mind, and soul. It improves health, brings love, and sustains life.

HERBS : ALTHEA, ROSE, BASIL, BORAGE, BLACK COHOSH, GINSENG, GOLDEN ROD, KAVA KAVA, LEMON BALM

OIL : ASSISTANCE

INCENSE : APPLE

Herb (Holy Plant)

   This Dzi assists the mind of the healer and will be of most benefit in the hands of a healer rather than a layman. The Herb Dzi attacks at the roots of disease rather than the symptoms. This Dzi can assist to remove the roots of diseases, and control their growth. This Dzi ensures health and is extremely rare. This Dzi assists the possessor to plant new roots of health, creating balance so that wellness can be maintained. It helps the possessor to have a healthy focus, and a healthy mind. Removing diseased attitudes, it replaces such with a healthier one.

The Herb Dzi assists in obtaining a wellness lifestyle. This Dzi is probably one of the strongest healing Dzi available. The Herb Dzi is often times considered too strong for the lay person.

HERBS : BAY, BASIL, PARSLEY, HIGH JOHN ROOT, ROSEMARY, GARLIC, SALT PETRE, RUE, CLOVES

OIL : PATH CLEARING

INCENSE : PALO SANTO

Horse

The Horse Dzi beads meaning advises you that all pathways have equal validity. Keeping this in mind will give you insight into the power and the glory of a unified family and humanity. Every human being must follow a pathway to empowerment before galloping upon the wings of destiny.

HERBS : LEMON PEEL, LOBELIA, MANDRAKE ROOT, LAVENDER, CALENDULA, CHAMOMILE, LEMON VERBENA, MEADOWSWEET, SPANISH MOSS

OIL : PATH CLEARING

INCENSE : SANDALWOOD

Insect (Felicity)

Also referred to as the Longevity Felicity bead, this Dzi looks like two headed insect. Observing the reverse side of the bead, you may find the bat. The Insect symbolizes the wonderful blessings of abundance, happiness, good fortune, and longevity.

HERBS : YERBA MATE, JASMINE, LIFE EVERLASTING, LANENDER, SKULLCAP, LEMON BALM, CHAPARREL, CASCARA SAGRADA, CATNIP

OIL : PATH CLEARING

INCENSE : PATCHOULI

Kwan Yin (Guan Yin)

Kwan Yin is also often times referred to as the Green Tara. She is believed to hear the cries of humans and attempts to assist with relieving the painful human experience. There is often another figure on the other side of the Kwan Yin. These second figures can be a wide variety of symbols. The Kwan Yin with her torch lit is known as the Zen Master, symbolizing the student achieving advancement toward enlightenment.

HERBS : CARAWAY SEED, CHILI PEPPER, KELP, MARSHMELLOW LEAF, MOTHERWORT, MYRRH, RASPBERRY LEAF, PALO SANTO, PASSION FLOWER

OIL : GIVE AND TAKE

INCENSE : CLOVE

Kylin (Qilin)

A unicorn of Chinese myth depicted with the tail of an ox and the legs and body of a deer that appears with the imminent arrival or passing of a sage or illustrious ruler. This is an amazing Dzi and should be treasured as an achievement when acquired.

HERBS : STAR ANISE, PALO SANTO, LAVENDER, ROSE, CHAMOMILE, CLOVES, SANDALWOOD, MINT, CINNAMON, CAMPHOR, SWEETGRASS

OIL : ENLIGHTENMENT

INCENSE : FRANKINCENSE AND MYRRH

Lightning and Mystic Knot

The Lightening and Mystic Knot Dzi help to withstand negative powers, to overcome obstacles, and to attract luck and wealth.

HERBS : RED SANDALWOOD, WHEAT, THYME, BLOODROOT, BLUE VERVAIN, DAMIANA, DEVILS CLAW, DITTANY OF CRETE, EGGSHELL

OIL : WEALTH ATTRACTING

INCENSE : DRAGONS BLOOD

Longevity Bottle

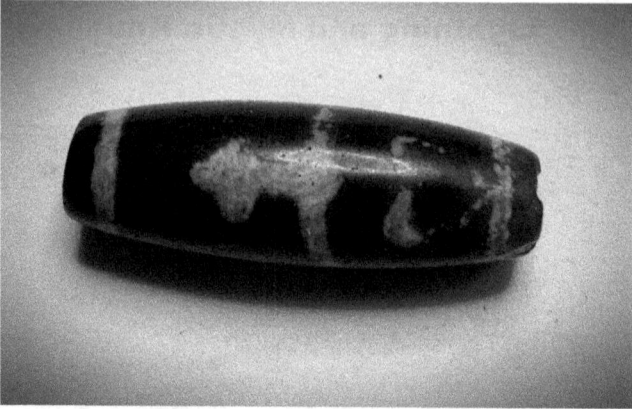

The Longevity Bottle bead helps the owner to make money and become healthier.

HERBS : ELDERBERRY, FENUGREEK SEED, FIVE FINGER GRASS, LEMON BALM, POPPY SEED, QUEEN OF THE MEADOW, SPEARMINT LEAF, ST. JOHNS WORT, YELLOW DOCK

OIL : WEALTH ATTRACTING

INCENSE : STRAWBERRY

Lotus

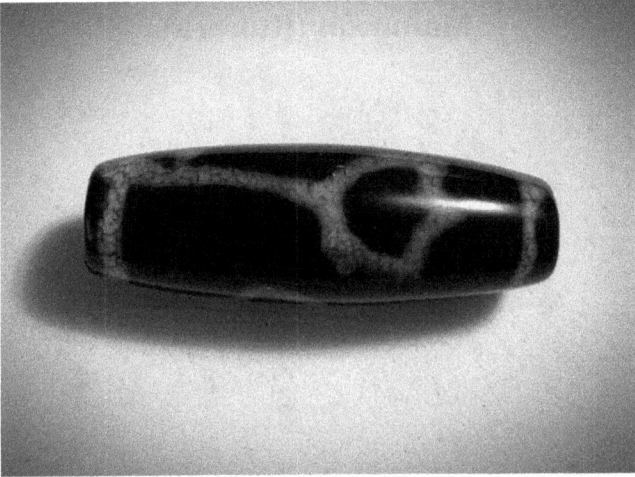

Lotus Dzi wishes for a pretty appearance and pleasant character with mental tranquility. It is believed that the Double Lotus Dzi bead will help to promote the purity, calmness, and charisma of its possessor. It will also energize the relationships of the possessor with the people around him and enhances his standing with them. This Dzi bestows attractiveness, calmness, and purity. It cleanses the body and mind, and enhances human relationships.

HERBS : BERGAMOT, DAMIANA, CATNIP, SANDALWOOD, JASMINE, LAVENDER, ROSEMARY, CINNAMON, PEPPERMINT

OIL : PATH CLEARING

INCENSE : SANDALWOOD

Mammon (Kubera)

This Dzi represents the Tibetan Wealth Deity Kubera's bestowing of wealth.

HERBS : SHEPHERDS PURSE, SKULLCAP, WHEAT, YELLOW DOCK, ALFALFA LEAF, BAT PETALS, BERGAMOT, CALAMUS ROOT, CHILI PEPPER

OIL : WEALTH ATTRACTING

INCENSE : MUSK

Mask

The Mask Dzi bead is a one of a kind for the enrichment of ones' life. The mask provides the possessor the ability to be whomever they choose to be at any given moment without thought. It grants the ability to "fit in" at any time. This is a highly prized Dzi.

HERBS : CELERY SEED, CINNAMON, CORRANDER SEED, DANDELION ROOT, DEER TONGUE, DITTANY OF CRETE, EYEBRIGHT, GINGER, HIGH JOHN ROOT

OIL : WEALTH ATTRACTING

INCENSE : LAVENDER

Medicine Buddha / Medicine

One function of the Medicine Buddhas is to assist with guilt the greatest disease and disease creator of all. Other functions of the Medicine Buddha are to bring back the laughter and the lightness. Medicine Buddhas help to take care of some of the dreary mundane day to day requirements that healers are responsible for in their personal lives so that their thoughts may be with healing of humanity.

HERBS : HIBISCUS, HYSSOP, JASMINE, LEMON PEEL, KAVA KAVA, MAJORAM LEAF, NUTMUG, MYRRH, FRANKINCENSE

OIL : PATH CLEARING

INCENSE : SAGE

Money Hook

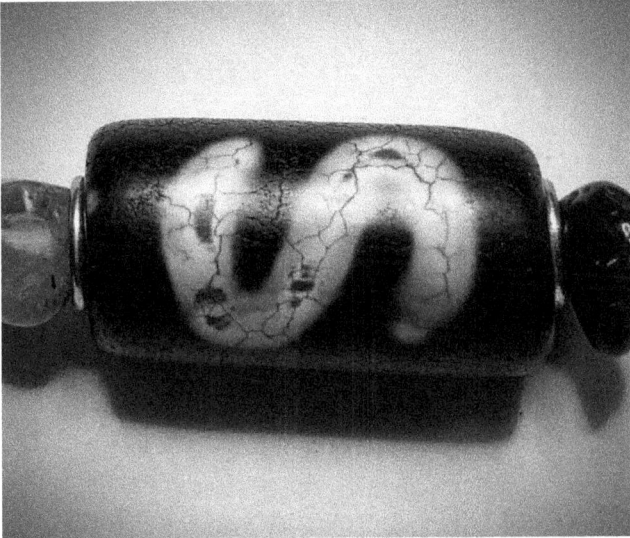

The Money Hook Dzi is called a Money Binding Hook. It resembles a dollar symbol. In addition to the aids of the Ruyi Money Hook, this hook brings the energy of internal power and intuition which helps to overcome the circumstances on the way to prosperity and financial success.

HERBS : ORANGE PEEL, RICE, SESAME SEED, SKULLCAP, ALFALFA LEAF, BLUE COHOSH, BUCKTHORN BARK, CALAMUS ROOT, CASCARA SAGRADA

OIL : WEALTH ATTRACTING

INCENSE : PATCHOULI

Monkey

The Monkey Dzi is a Divine messenger, who blesses marriage, bearing children and who protects against negative entities.

HERBS : BUTTERCUP, CHAMOMILE, CUMIN, DEVILS SHOWSTRING, DRAGONS BLOOD, ELDER FLOWERS, FAVA BEANS, MASTER OF THE WOODS, SAGE

OIL : WEALTH ATTRACTING

INCENSE : MAGNOLIA

Monsignor / Big Man / Da Ren

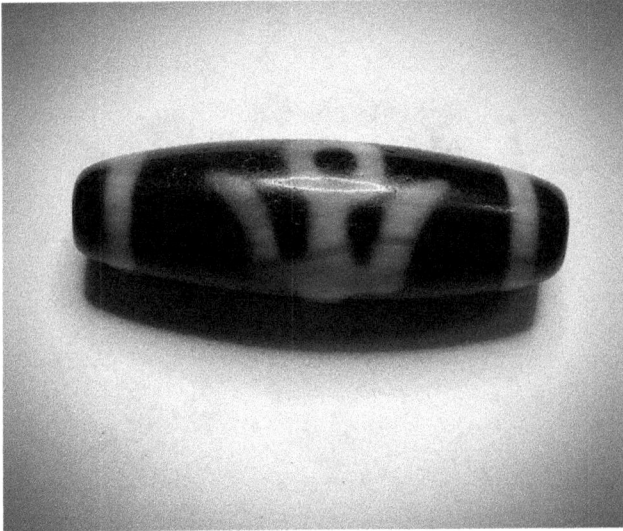

The Monsignor Dzi is believed to render mental support for hard-workers, and removes obstacles, or bad luck ahead. It helps to keep the mind agile and healthy, while also assisting with memory and cognition.

HERBS : ELDERBERRY, GALANGAL, GARLIC, GINGER, CINNAMON, ONION, LEMONGRASS, LOVAGE ROOT, MANDRAKE ROOT

OIL : PATH CLEARING

INCENSE : CHANDAN

Mountain, Peak, or Hill

The symbol of the hills, peaks, or mountains are likened to great support as afforded by the mountains mammoth stability, along with the elimination of bad luck and obstacles. This Dzi can assist in creating all forms of support for almost any situation. It helps to impart strength and focus for accomplishing that which needs to be done.

HERBS : LEMONGRASS, LEMON PEEL, MARSHMELLOW LEAF, ONION, MUSTARD SEED, MULLEIN, NUTMEG, PAPRIKA, SULFUR

OIL : PATH CLEARING

INCENSE : MYRRH

Nectar Bottle

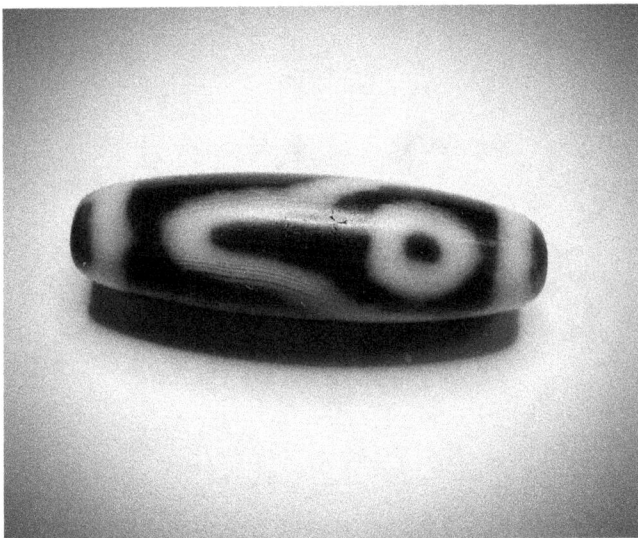

The Nectar Bottle Dzi looks like a bottle. It prevents death due to back luck, perfects your virtues establishment, helps obtain wealth and gain longevity.

HERBS : WHITE OAK BARK, WHITE SAGE, TARRAGON, VERVAIN, TURMERIC, AGRIMONY, ANGELICA, CLOVES, COLTSFOOT

OIL : WEALTH ATTRACTING

INCENSE : LILY

Om

It is the power of the word, sacral sound, primary mantra, power of the Heavens, support of Higher Forces, mystic power and protection. This bead may be found in alternative forms.

HERBS : BAY, BASIL, ROSEMARY, RUE, ONION, GARLIC, PARSLEY, CLOVES, GINGER

OIL : ATTENTION

INCENSE : VIOLET

Ox

The Ox Dzi is a symbol of abundance and manifesting goals.

HERBS : CLEAVER, DILL SEED, HOREHOUND, JUNIPER, MISTLETOE, ARROWROOT, BILBERRY LEAF, BONESET, CATS CLAW

OIL : WEALTH ATTRACTING

INCENSE : SAGE

Phoenix Eye (Mandy the Phoenix)

The Phoenix Eye Dzi will help you to see the mysterious light of Tibetan stone Cintamani – the heart of all things. It is considered that Dzi with such pattern restore health, grant long life and luck, and eliminate fuss.

HERBS : CARAWAY SEED, CATNIP, ROSE, LAVENDER, CALENDULA, CHAMOMILE, MINT, CINNAMON

OIL : PATH CLEARING

INCENSE : COCONUT

Pig

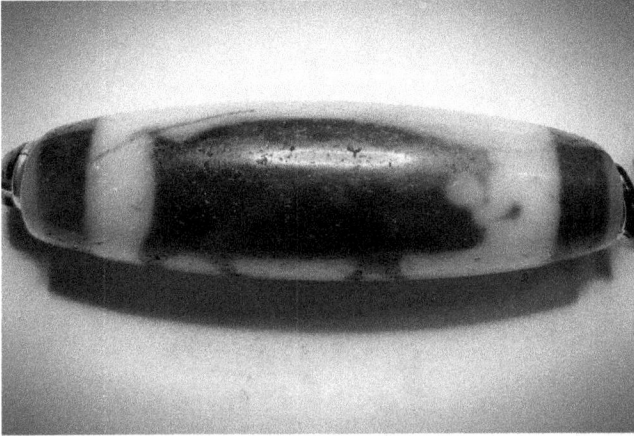

The Pig Dzi bead will bring Generosity and Wealth.

HERBS : BURDOCK ROOT, COMFREY, COLTSFOOT, CRAMP BARK, ELECAMPANE, GOLDEN ROD, GRAVEL ROOT, HORSE CHESTNUT, GUINEA PEPPER

OIL : WEALTH ATTRACTING

INCENSE : VANILLA

Rabbit

The Rabbit Dzi symbolizes fertility, family and new life. It deals primarily with abundance, comfort, and vulnerability.

HERBS : GUM ARABIC, HIBISCUS, LEMON BALM, LICORICE ROOT, LOBELIA, MARSHMELLOW ROOT, MEADOWSWEET, MUGWORT, ORRIS

OIL : EXPANSION

INCENSE : STRAWBERRY

Rat

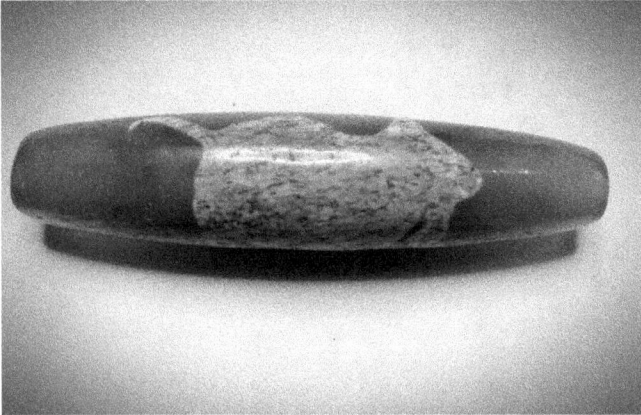

The Rat Dzi can communicate with God to predict good or bad luck.

HERBS : PEPPERMINT, WITCH HAZEL, BAY LEAF, BLUE VERVAIN, CELERY SEED, CINQUEFOIL, CRAMP BARK, DANDELION ROOT, DITTANY OF CRETE

OIL : PATH CLEARING

INCENSE : AMBER

Rooster

The Rooster Dzi bead draws good luck, prosperity and overall health to both you and your situation or projects.

HERBS : DAMIANA, EUCALYPTUS LEAF, FIVE FINGER GRASS, HYSSOP, JEZEBEL, LIFE EVERLASTING, LOBELIA, MOTHERWORT, ONION

OIL : WEALTH ATTRACTING

INCENSE : MYRRH

Ruyi (As you Wish Bead)

This Dzi offers power, acknowledgment, and authority to aid you in coping with any issue with maximum advantage.

HERBS : MUSK, OATSTRAW, ORRIS, PERIWINKLE, SAGE, CHAMOMILE, CINQUEFOIL, COLTSFOOT, HYSSOP

OIL : WEALTH ATTRACTING

INCENSE : CINNAMON

Snake

The Snake Dzi brings wisdom in study and science, the making of correct decisions, as well as bringing mystical abilities.

HERBS : RUE, HIGH JOHN ROOT, JASMINE, LOVAGE ROOT, MINT, FRANKINCENSE, MYRRH, PAU D'ARCO, PALO SANTO

OIL : ASSISTANCE

INCENSE : CLOVE

Spider

The Spider Dzi weaves its' webs to catch luck. At the same time it throws the net over the enemy. It also helps to fulfill creative plans.

HERBS: BLADDERWACK, MARSHMELLOW ROOT, MARJORAM LEAF, TURMERIC, VERVAIN, ROSE, CALENDULA, CALEA ZACATECHICHI, PLANTAIN LEAF

OIL: WEALTH ATTRACTING

INCENSE: OPIUM

Star (Cross or Coin)

The Star Dzi bead may appear as a five point star or simply a filled in dot. Is the symbol of the natural law of the universe, and accumulates your good virtue.

HERBS : PARSLEY, PENNYROYAL, OREGANO, POKE ROOT, PINE, SHEEP SORREL, TARRAGON, VALERIAN ROOT, WHITE WILLOW BARK

OIL : PATH CLEARING

INCENSE : CHERRY

Striped

Usually one stripe or band means healing abilities. This Dzi is also used to craft a Tiger Tooth Dzi bead necklace.

HERBS : ACACIA, ASAFOETIDA, BASIL, GUM ARABIC, HOREHOUND, BILBERRY LEAF, BLOODROOT, VALERIAN ROOT, WHITE OAK BARK

OIL : PATH CLEARING

INCENSE : MUSK

Sun and Moon

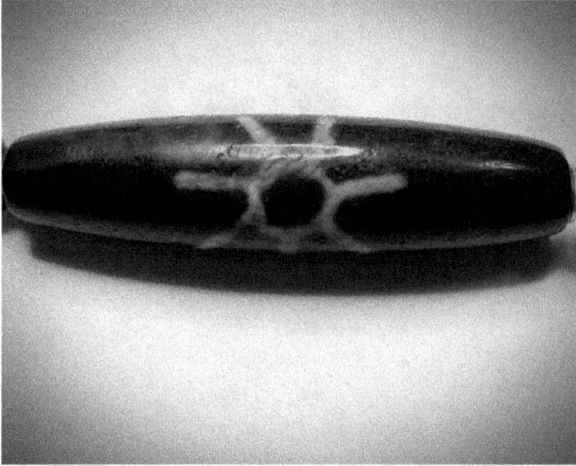

Two luminaries on one bead – is a simultaneously simple and complicated symbol. This is for both clarity, which the Dzi gives to understand what is happening, and two basic energies of the universe, yin and yang, which it harmonizes. This is a specific Dzi, it helps its owner to realize his mission, to plan the way of self-actualization and successfully follow it. This Dzi will help those who are pure of heart, sincere, who look for truth, and who are ready to share energy. The bead itself will become the source of energy, that's why its possessor should not be afraid of exhausting.

HERBS : SWEETGRASS, WINTERGREEN, BORAGE, BLACK KOHOSH, BLUE COHOSH, CATS SLAW, CAMPHOR, CINQUEFOIL, CINNAMON

OIL : EXPANSION

INCENSE : FRANKINCENSE

Sun Moon Star

The Sun and the Moon balance the energies of opposite poles. The star lights up the way to purpose. This Dzi promotes enlightenment in all the spheres of life. It will help to find your way and live in harmony with the external world and yourself.

HERBS : CLEAVER, CLUB MOSS, COPAL ORO, CORKSILK, ROSE HIPS, JUNIPER, KELP, MEADOWSWEET, PENNYROYAL

OIL : EXPANSION

INCENSE : SAGE

Swastika (WanZi)

The Swastika (WanZi) can help in aiding the proceedings to benefit the possessor, or to go easier on the possessor of this Dzi. If the possessor is in tune with this Dzi it can help to protect them from being in the wrong place at the wrong time.

HERBS : BUCKTHORN BARK, BLESSED THISTLE, LEMONGRASS, MARSHMELLOW LEAF, NETTLE LEAF, ELECAMPANE, GALANGAL, GOLDENSEAL ROOT, RUE

OIL : WEALTH ATTRACTING

INCENSE : NAG CHAMPA

Tara

The Tara Dzi can help to avoid misfortune, to protect against enemies, jinx, and to get justice. It will give a chance to reach new frontiers in science to those who study.

HERBS : ROSE HIPS, RUE, SANDALWOOD, SAW PALMETTO, CHAPARREL, CHILI PEPPER, CLUS MOSS, DEVILS CLAW, DRAGONS BLOOD

OIL : WEALTH ATTRACTING

INCENSE : LILY

Tiger Tooth

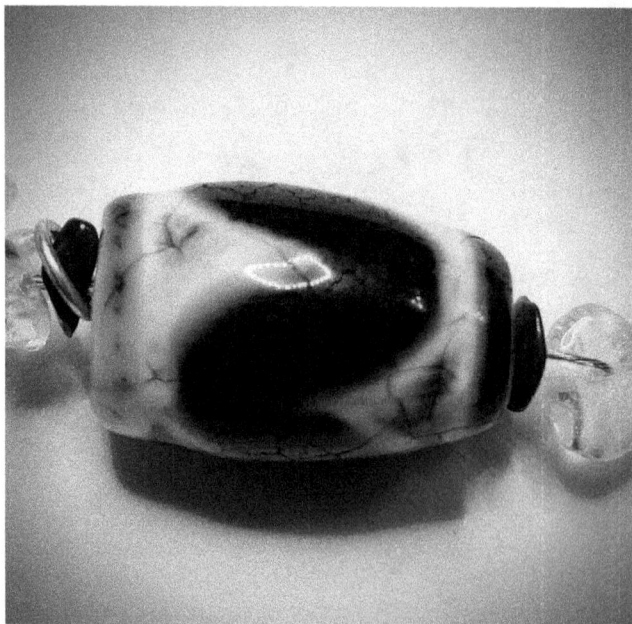

Tiger Teeth on a Dzi will almost look like a wave pattern. The waves will be deeper and more pointed or chiseled than the wave pattern is. The Tiger's Teeth can be combined with other patterns to intensify the designs. Tiger's Teeth Dzis can also come shaped like a tooth. Culturing a firm and persistent will, the Tigers Tooth removes frustrations along the way, and guarantees for you a healthy life. This Dzi can aid with follow through and will-power. It can help its possessor to follow through. It also assists in focusing on what's important thus allowing for more free time for true relaxation, free of guilt and stress. Tiger Teeth Dzi can help the possessor with concentration, determination, and completion.

HERBS : ACACIA, ASAFOETIDA, BASIL, GUM ARABIC, HOREHOUND, BILBERRY LEAF, BLOODROOT, VALERIAN ROOT, WHITE OAK BARK

OIL : PATH CLEARING

INCENSE : MUSK

Tiger Teeth (Double)

Having Multi-Band Designs with Two Layers of Tiger's Teeth inscriptions, designed in a unique pattern, these Dzis double or magnify the intensity of the Tiger Teeth Dzi bead. This Dzi helps to promote spiritual strength, cleansing of evil and obstacles, and attraction of all auspicious signs for the owner. This Dzi is widely sought for its spiritual properties. It is believed to possess six times the spiritual strength of the normal Tiger's Tooth, due to the multi-band designs.

HERBS : ACACIA, ASAFOETIDA, BASIL, GUM ARABIC, HOREHOUND, BILBERRY LEAF, BLOODROOT, VALERIAN ROOT, WHITE OAK BARK

OIL : PATH CLEARING

INCENSE : MUSK

Turtle Back (Tortoise)

The Turtle Back Dzi ensures longevity in good health. The Turtle Back Motif Dzi is for cultivating good health; leading to longevity, and strengthening determination in work accomplishment. It renders protection from sickness caused by spirits and gives bodily protection. It is believed that the Turtle Back Dzi is able to protect the wearer from sickness and diseases. Furthermore, the bead is believed to be able to promote good health and speedy recovery from sickness.

HERBS : TARRAGON, VERVAIN, KELP, LEMON VERBENA, LIFE EVERLASTING, MISTLETOE, ELDERBERRY, EUCALYPTUS LEAF, FEVERFEW

OIL : ATTENTION

INCENSE : PALO SANTO

Universal Spiral

This ancient symbol, which combines the universal harmony with the deepest desires of its possessor. It is also a maze – a mysterious symbol of space, which came to us from the depth of the centuries and can be met on all the continents. This Dzi assists in striving, tirelessness in purposeful achievements, long life, and prosperity to its possessor. It may aid in conceiving a child and is known for fertility. The Universal Spiral represents perpetual motion, filling you with pure positive energy to move you forward.

HERBS : LIFE EVERLASTING, FENUGREEK SEED, FENNEL SEED, OLIVE LEAF, SAGE, CHILI PEPPER, CORRANDER SEED, CUMIN, ORRIS

OIL : WEALTH ATTRACTING

INCENSE : CANNABIS

Wave (Fountain of Abundance)

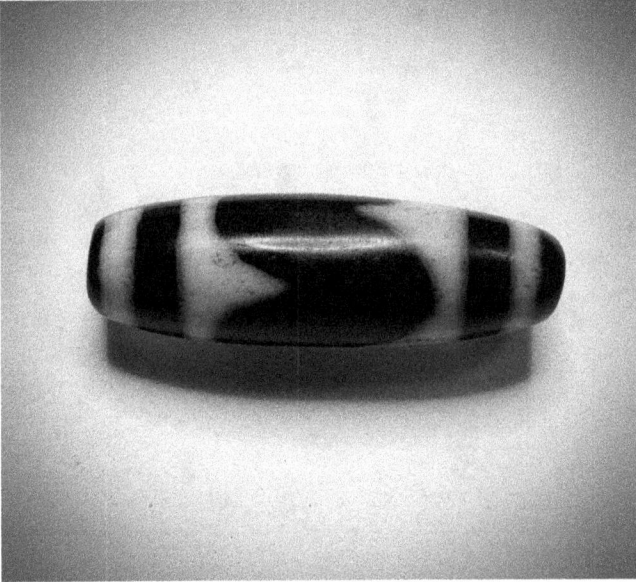

The Wave Dzi grants prosperity, happiness, power, and protection. The Wave Dzi is also the image of our feelings, which this bead helps to harness, to align and focus them.

HERBS : PARSLEY, PAU D'ARCO, POPPY SEED, RED CLOVER, SHEPHERDS PURSE, STRAWEBERRY LEAF, YERBA MATE, WINTERGREEN, ALFALFA LEAF

OIL : PATH CLEARING

INCENSE : DRAGONS BLOOD

Yin and Yang (Taiji)

The Yin and Yang Dzi will help its possessor to order their energy, to connect to a bottomless reservoir of the universe, and even to get to the mystery of space, provided that the possessor improves himself.

HERBS : ALLSPICE, CLOVE, BUTTERCUP, CARAWAY SEED, BALSAM FIR, BAY LEAF, JASMINE, SPANISH MOSS, PLANTAIN LEAF

OIL : PATH CLEARING

INCENSE : ALOE VERA

Vajra (Dorje / Diamond)

The Vajra Dzi assists in bringing to light all that is beautiful or dormant within the self. It allows the owner to live in a state of beauty and brilliance.

HERBS : POPPY SEED, QUEEN OF THE MEADOW, PALO SANTO, PENNYROYAL, PEPPERMINT, DEER TONGUE, DILL SEED, COPAL ORO, CHICORY ROOT

OIL : PATH CLEARING

INCENSE : ROSE

Zhao Cai Jin Bao

This Dzi looks like a tree with 2 round legs at the bottom. Zhao Cai Jin Bao translates as, "money and treasures will be plentiful" and "attracts wealth and treasure". Zhao meaning, "attract".

HERBS : RICE, SESAME SEED, FAVA BEANS, FLAX SEED, GRAVEL ROOT, OATSTRAW, ORANGE PEEL, WHEAT, BERGAMOT

OIL : WEALTH ATTRACTING

INCENSE : CITRUS

One-Eye (Goat Eye)

The Goat Eye Dzi is believed to bring wearers light, hope, and life-long happiness. Wearing this Dzi aids in helping its possessor to be brave, determined, strong, self-confident, and help them realize their dreams. This is the Dzi for hope.

HERBS : BARBERRY, BAY LEAF, CALAMUS ROOT, CARAWAY SEED, AGRIMONY, ANGELICA, WORDWOOD, WINTERGREEN, HYSSOP

OIL : PATH CLEARING

INCENSE : VANILLA

Two-Eye

Two-eyed Dzi brings harmony in personal relationships and contributes to a successful career. It is believed this Dzi is good for balance in life. This is the Dzi for Family.

HERBS : CHAMOMILE, CATNIP, ROSE, DAMIANA, CINNAMON, GINGER, MINT, BASIL, CLOVES

OIL : WEALTH ATTRACTING

INCENSE : MYRRH

Three-Eye

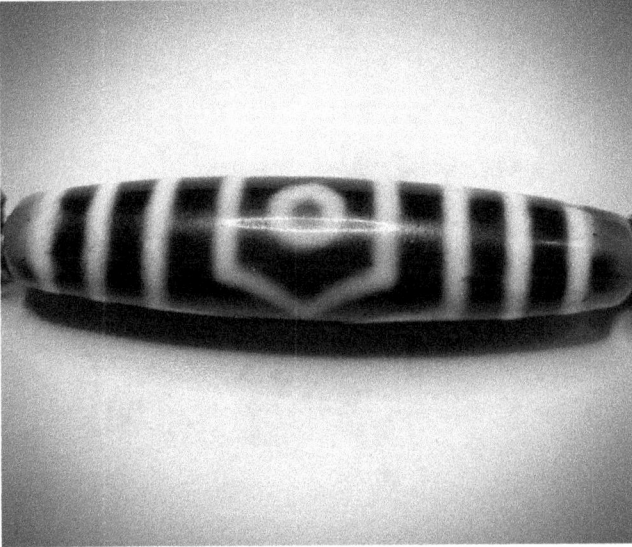

Three-eyed Dzis are believed to bring heavenly wealth.

HERBS : HORSE CHESTNUT, HIGH JOHN ROOT, JEZEBEL, WINTERGREEN, CINNAMON, ALLSPICE, ALFALFA LEAF, WHEAT, OATSTRAW

OIL : WEALTH ATTRACTING

INCENSE : JASMINE

Four-Eye

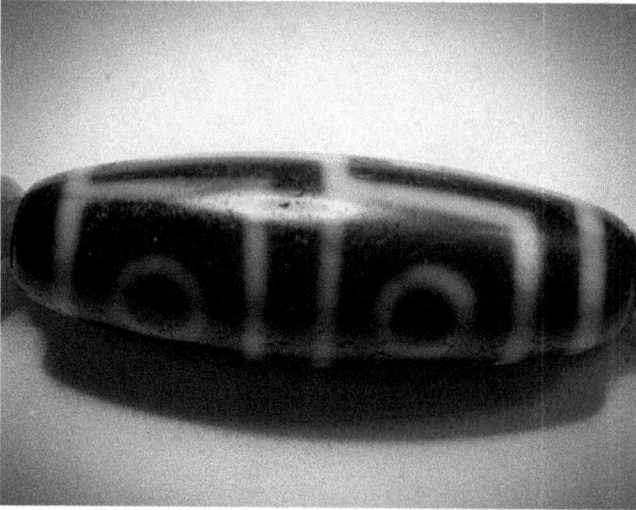

Four-eyed Dzi helps to clear obstacles, overcome negative influences, release human suffering, and keep anger under control. It also brings longevity. This is the Good Fortune Dzi.

HERBS : JASMINE, PEPPERMINT, LAVENDER, ROSEMARY, ORANGE PEEL, LEMON PEEL, FRANKINCENSE, ELECAMPANE, SAGE

OIL : ASSISTANCE

INCENSE : SANDALWOOD

Five-Eye

Five-eyed Dzi assists the person who wears the Dzi to obtain whatever he/she desires and brings endless happiness. The five-eyed Lightening Dzi; In addition of the symbolism of the five-eyed DZI, it helps the possessor to overcome obstacles in his/her life. This is the wealth and prosperity Dzi.

HERBS : SAW PALMETTO, SESAME SEED, CHAPARREL, CINQUEFOIL, CLOVES, COUCHGRASS, CUMIN, EGGSHELL, PATCHOULI

OIL : PATH CLEARING

INCENSE : SAGE

Six-Eye

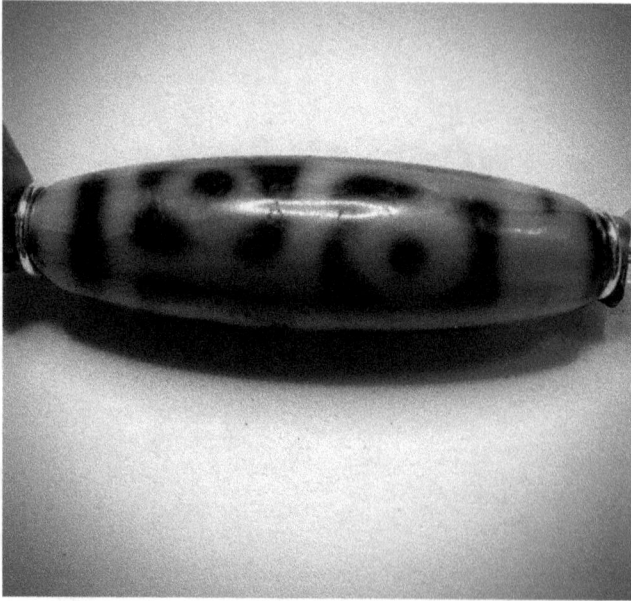

Six-eyed is believed to bring elimination of the sadness and sufferings in life, and to accumulate knowledge of the middle way, while obtaining a loving nature. It helps the possessor to find the root of happiness and good karma through joyous effort and correct efforts. This is the Dzi for perfect harmony.

HERBS : AMBER GUM, ARROWROOT, CALAMUS ROOT, CATNIP, DANDELION LEAF, CEDAR, SENNA, FAVA BEANS, FEVERFEW

OIL : PATH CLEARING

INCENSE : VANILLA

Seven-Eye

Seven-eyed Dzi represents the seven stars of the big dipper in the universe. The Dzi should help one to achieve perfection, glory, fame, relationships, careers, fame, wealth, and a healthy life. This is the abundance and good luck Dzi.

HERBS : FAVA BEANS, FLAX SEED, NUTMEG, MOTHERWORT, LEMON BALM, YARROW, BAT PETALS, PASSION FLOWER, STRAWBERRY LEAF

OIL : WEALTH ATTRACTING

INCENSE : CINNAMON

Eight-Eye

Eight-eyed Dzi bead creates harmony and fulfillment in one's mind. This Dzi also protects the wearer against calamities. This is the Dzi to guarantee the correct path.

HERBS : FRANKINCENCE, MYRRH, PALO SANTO, BARBERRY, BAY LEAF, WOOD BOTANY, BONESET, BLADDERWACK, BLESSLE THISTLE

OIL : PATH CLEARING

INCENSE : ALOE VERA

Nine-Eye

Nine-Eyed Dzi is the emperor Dzi. This Dzi is also a wealth Dzi by the local Tibetan people. Possessing a nine-eye Dzi helps people expand intelligence and wisdom, obtain ability, enhance power and purify negative energy. It helps the investors with successful development of new ideas in rolling in wealth.

HERBS : BLUE COHOSH, BLOODROOT, VERVAIN, WHITE OAK BARK, WHITE SAGE, LEMON VERBENA, LEMONGRASS, LOVAGE ROOT, MARJORAM LEAF

OIL : WEALTH ATTRACTING

INCENSE : FRANKINCENSE

Ten-Eye

Ten-eyed Dzi is a symbol of perfection in everything. It helps the possessor to have a happy relationship with their partner and it aids in removing obstacles in the area of career development. This is the perfection Dzi.

HERBS : LICORICE ROOT, LEMON BALM, WHEAT, SWEETGRASS, BLACK COHOSH, YELLOW DOCK, ASTER, ORRIS, PERIWINKLE

OIL : PATH CLEARING

INCENSE : CHERRY

Eleven-Eye

Eleven-Eye Dzi is almost the same as the Nine-Eye Dzi bead. Wearing jewelry with the 11 eye Dzi can strongly enhance the powers of the Dzi and helps to purify negative chi.

HERBS : MARJORAM LEAF, MISTLETOE, OAT TOPS, EUCALYPTUS LEAF, SAGE, COPAL ORO, DANDELION LEAF, CAMPHOR, ARROWROOT

OIL : PATH CLEARING

INCENSE : SUPER HIT

Twelve-Eye

Twelve-Eye Dzi is believed to purify one's karma; to turn over bad luck, to increase wisdom and virtue, to promote social and networking skills, to clear obstructions in career development, to enhance one's charisma, and to ensure happy relationships. It stands for courage, fame, and reputation. This is the fearlessness Dzi.

HERBS : PINE, POPPY SEED, QUEEN OF THE MEADOW, STAR ANISE, GUINEA PEPPER, JEZEBEL, JUNIPER, ANISE SEED, ALFALFA

OIL : PATH CLEARING

INCENSE : CLOVE

Thirteen-Eye

Thirteen-Eye Dzi is believed to promote mental and body tranquility. This is the virtue Dzi.

HERBS : ACACIA, ARGIMONY, ALLSPICE, ALTHEA, ALUM, AMBER GUM, ANGELIA, ARROWROOT, SAGE

OIL : PATH CLEARING

INCENSE : CANNABIS

Fourteen-Eye

Fourteen-Eye Dzi protects the mind from clutter and helps with karma issues.

HERBS : BURDOCK ROOT, CALAMUS ROOT, CUMIN, CLOVES, COUCHGRASS, CRUEL MAN OF THE WOODS, CELERY SEED, CELERY FLAKES, RUE

OIL : PATH CLEARING

INCENSE : CHANDAN

Fifteen-Eye

Fifteen-Eye Dzi is believed to imbue wearer with auspicious Heaven's Luck, to clear life's obstacles, to ensure smoothness in your undertakings, to promises windfall luck, and to attract good opportunities. This is the Dzi for luck.

HERBS : SESAME SEED, SENNA, ROSE, FENNEL SEED, FLAX SEED, GINKOGOTO KOLA, MUSTARD SEED, OREGANO

OIL : WEALTH ATTRACTING

INCENSE : AYURVEDA

Eighteen-Eye

Eighteen Eye Dzi protects against compulsions and obsessions. Those with addiction or bad habits and vices, ex: (sexual addictions, drug abuse, alcoholism, gambling etc). will find the Eighteen Eye Tibetan Dzi helpful.

HERBS : PALO SANTO, BAT NUTS, ASAFOETIDA, BASIL, BAY LEAF, WORMWOOD, BLESSED THISTLE, BONESET, WHITE SAGE

OIL : PATH CLEARING

INCENSE : SANDALWOOD

Nineteen-Eye

Nineteen-Eye Dzi enhances the owner's ability to manifest & materialize the necessary things in one's life.

HERBS : BLUE COHOSH, LEMON PEEL, WOOD SORREL, YELLOW DOCK, BAY LEAF, BERGAMOT, PAPRIKA, CINNAMON, WHITE WILLOW BARK

OIL : WEALTH ATTRACTING

INCENSE : CITRUS

Twenty One-Eye

   Twenty One-Eye Dzi offers the wearer the greatest magic, strength, power, health, and wealth. This Dzi enhances one's ability to help others in restoring their life.

HERBS : LOVAGE ROOT, CINNAMON, CRAMP BARK, DEVILS SHOESTRING, ECHINACEA, CAMPHOR, CATS CLAW, MINT, ORANGE PEEL

OIL : PATH CLEARING

INCENSE : CINNAMON

Twenty Seven-Eye

Twenty Seven-Eye Dzi is believed to bring good windfall luck from all directions. It helps one to succeed in their job and in getting money that will help maintain balance, as well as help increase health.

HERBS : CARAWAY SEED, GRAVEL ROOT, CALAMUS ROOT, CLAENDULA, DILL SEED, PURPLE DEAD NETTLE, RED SANDALWOOD, GUINEA PEPPER, STRAWBERRY LEAF

OIL : WEALTH ATTRACTING

INCENSE : MYRRH

Twenty Eight-Eye

Twenty Eight-Eye Dzi ensures easy flow through life. It allows things to flow smoothly in and out of your life.

HERBS : HIGH JOHN ROOT, JUNIPER, ALTHEA, AMBER GUM, ANISE SEED, LAVENDER, KAVA KAVA, WHITE OAK BARK, PASSION FLOWER, PENNYROYAL

OIL : PATH CLEARING

INCENSE : LAVENDER

Thirty Six-Eye

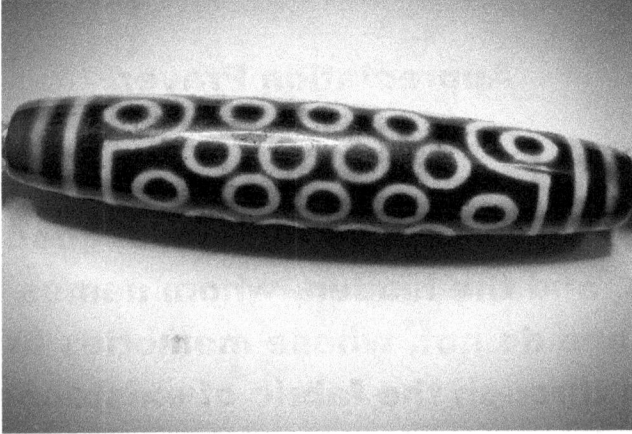

Thirty Six-Eye Dzi grants luck, fortune, and longevity. It will bring you good luck, wealthiness, and long life. It is the Fortune God in Tibetan Buddhism. It is VERY hard to find.

HERBS : PATCHOULI, PENNYROYAL, PEPPERMINT, BAT PETALS, BAY LEAF, BALSAM FIR, YERBA MATE, BORAGE, LIFE EVERLASTING

OIL : WEALTH ATTRACTING

INCENSE : FRANKINCENSE

PRAYERS
-Special Gift From Me to You-

Appreciation Prayer

I call to you, and ask that you hear my voice. Creator, ancestors, gods, good spirits, and the hidden, whom names I both know and do not, whose memories are woven through the fabric of existence. Whose bones lie beneath this land in which we have conquered and ruled.

I come to you, across the many spans of time, to the beginning of our existence.

I love you. I am grateful. I thank you for accepting me before I came into this life and thank you for protecting me now, and for extending it to my surroundings.

I ask that you continue to protect me fiercely. Open new paths for success, stability, peace, and prosperity for my existence. Help me live a full, bountiful, and rich life.

Thank you for your sacrifices. Thank you for your infinite wisdom. To be rich is to have acquired the lessons of gratitude. I pray that each of you are protected, and liberated from your pains and traumas. I pray for your healing, as you are healed I am also. I pray that you are healed both inwardly and outwardly through the timelines, so that our entire lineage may be lifted up in glory. May that healing flow through every branch of our family tree, touching every descendant along its way, into abundance and beyond. In God's name, AMEN.

Appreciation Prayer II

I call to you, and ask that you hear my voice. Creator, ancestors, gods, good spirits, and the hidden, whom names I both know and do not, whose memories are woven through the fabric of existence. Whose bones lie beneath this land in which we have conquered and ruled.

Hear me and shower me with love as I honor you.

All that is of good, sleeping in the waters and the earth, awaken and hear me. Ancestors, who oversee us from the heavens, lingering in the celestial spheres, patrolling the worlds to prevent collapse. Descend and shower me with love as I honor you. Those of who are my last lives, who carry my memories of my times before light flickers, bring them to me and remind me how to honor myself. Imbue me with righteous power. Make my protections unparalleled. Share with me your knowledge. From this, let us weave miracles together. May our family, in its entirety, elevate to splendor. I honor you, here and across realms to where time has no dominion. May this bond never die. I am grateful for you, and for everything you have conquered since the beginning of existence - thank you. In God's name, AMEN.

I call to you, and ask that you hear my voice. Creator, ancestors, gods, good spirits, and the hidden, whom names I both know and do not, whose memories are woven through the fabric of existence. Whose bones lie beneath this land in which we have conquered and ruled.

I am not stuck. I have the power to supersede myself.

I ask to now be bestowed with the always expanding presence of wealth. Money, like vines from a tree, come wrap your branches around my life and provide me the fruit of coins and currency. Just as the ocean is generous with fish, overtake me with the currents of wealth from horizon to horizon.

Follow me, wealth, everywhere I go. Stick to me like a shadow. I am a magnet for wealth and all the financial luck it brings. Empower me with the freedom the currency of money provides.

I draw an abundance of money from every thoughtful breath I take. Each word of gratitude I speak, may it be returned in wealth as I have never known.

Wealth, you are my friend, my dearest of blessings - come stay with me and provide me with stability, safety, and freedom.

I will to attract wealth, and it cling to me the way the planets cling to their rotations around the sun. My actions and movements are prosperous, always leading me to abundance. I pray that my currency is unlimited, free of false beliefs that limit me, free from fears and negativity. Shall it find me in all ways I do not yet see.

I embrace wealth positively and without hesitation. I ask that money flow my direction, so I may better my life and the lives of others, as many as possible along my journey. Money, cork my financial drains and turn them into an overflow, into opportunities for financial increase and advancement. Allow me foresight so that I may halt wasteful spending, prevent theft, and advert financial mishaps. Protect my assets. As the oldest human exchange of trust, the authority of worth, wealth and value, know that I have earned this trust, and I ask that you pour your riches into every aspect of my existence. I am ready, direct the currency of wealth to me uninhibited, boundless, and never ending. In God's name, AMEN.

Path Clearing

I call to you, and ask that you hear my voice. Creator, ancestors, gods, good spirits, and the hidden, whom names I both know and do not, whose memories are woven through the fabric of existence. Whose bones lie beneath this land in which we have conquered and ruled.

Separate me from all of my unhealthy, parasitic, stagnant romantic, platonic, and sexual relationships. Sever these cords from my soul, like a knife through butter. Do not allow me accept life meagerly, as a common beggar would. Prohibit me from accepting inferior treatment, abuse, manipulation, or detachment. Cut the energy off from these tendencies and exorcise them from my life. In their place, allow longevity, compassion, rich and sensitive love, and utter sexual satisfaction to devour me. I am whole as I am, and will not negotiate my values to please others. I honor myself daily, knowing who I am and what I offer. I ask that you help clear the obstacles that block my path. Remove them, and bind them; casting them into the depths forever and ever. Clear this path for me, a to b with as little resistance as possible while reminding me of the lessons I have learned for the knowledge of the power of gratitude. I am humbly thankful for you now, to be here with me, to assist me on my way. I know to ask you when I need the assistance, and I am asking you for that guidance now. Come to me, help me, so that I may be of assistance to every soul with ears to hear as I continue my journey in peace without hamper. Thank you, I am grateful. In God's name, AMEN.

Revocation

I call to you, and ask that you hear my voice. Creator, ancestors, gods, good spirits, and the hidden, whom names I both know and do not, whose memories are woven through the fabric of existence. Whose bones lie beneath this land in which we have conquered and ruled.

Bear witness and assist me in expelling evil decrees from within the boundaries of my reality. May the effervescent power of righteousness be woven into me, all of my days. May I move forward in wealth, abundance, and prosperity; free from hindrance of evil influence.

All pettiness, jealousies, and false accusations against me, I revoke you. May my enemies' mouths be sewn shut and their throats bound in silence. Any malicious attacks in any form against my life, my livelihood and my loved ones, I revoke you. I bind you and cast you into the darkness from which you came. Confusion, anxieties, weaknesses, heaviness of body and spirit, sleep terrors, unhealthy attachments spoken against me, I revoke you. Vile and negative forces, energy vampires, and all parasitic spirits in every manifested form attempting to use me as food, I revoke you. I halt that energy transference NOW. I forbid any links to me, traces, and essences, and I scatter them to the winds like angry ashes. I paralyze the works of my enemies, and I rain flaming daggers upon their vehicles of operations by all means I am capable. I revoke their hateful words and deeds so that they may not as much as feast upon their own diseased spirit. They are no longer able to retain that negative energy toward me, the ties broken now, at this moment without further thought. All these unwanted presences are hereby forever dismissed from my existence, my family's existence, and by any other means they are able to invoke harm towards me. I'm encircled in an unrelenting whirlwind of divine and ancestral protection from this moment forward. In God's name, AMEN.

Serendipity

I call to you, and ask that you hear my voice. Creator, ancestors, gods, good spirits, and the hidden, whom names I both know and do not, whose memories are woven through the fabric of existence. Whose bones lie beneath this land in which we have conquered and ruled.

I pray for the wind of serendipity to whirl itself into every fabric of my existence, twisting and coiling away from flickers of misfortune. Serendipity, I summon you to me. I come before you and ask of you to extend a gracious hand over all of my efforts and my endeavors. Do not allow deficit to linger over any aspect my life and fill those holes with unbelievable fortune.

My pantry is layered with soul-filling food, my mouth with words of honey. My wallet shines a glittering pool of prosperity. My health improves every day I can open my eyes with gratitude. My lovers beckon for me, hungry with desires to accommodate me.

Serendipity, you were the ignition that birthed creation. The spark, at the proper moment, yielding everything in its entirety. You are the first breath that fills the newborn's lungs. The divine exhale that awakened life. You are the essence permeating all space, unwavering, both lovely and capricious, forever the equalizer in all affairs to both the living and the spirit. You make beggars out of kings and kings out of beggars. You are the master of reversal, so I ask for you to turn away all bad luck. I ask you to bless me, encompassing me, at every angle, at all times. May your ways cover and shield my family as well, so they will neither go without. Serendipity, may your gracious ways prevail yet again. In God's name, AMEN.

Chronic Illness

I call to you, and ask that you hear my voice. Creator, ancestors, gods, good spirits, and the hidden, whom names I both know and do not, whose memories are woven through the fabric of existence. Whose bones lie beneath this land in which we have conquered and ruled.

I pray that my vessel regains its strength as a warrior. I pray that it will find ways with your assistance, for it to heal itself gently and thoroughly. If there is to be pain in this process, I ask that it be light, because every wound on my path to healing is stitched with golden love, righteousness, and just.

I pray that I'm lifted from depression, that my mind is clear and elevated so that I may be of my greatest potential. I pray that my mind does not wage war with itself, rather remaining strong in faith. I pray that my mind does not wage war with my body, knowing that we are as one within the constructs of this reality. I pray that the temple in which my spirit dwells moves in divine order, harmoniously throughout eternity, regardless of the vessel in which my soul travels.

My body loves me, as I am grateful for its use in this lifetime.
My body shields me from death, as I honor it for its service.
My body is enduring, because I maintain it to best of my ability.
My mind is resilient, for I know the boundaries of this reality, and respect them.

My spirit is in Harmony, for I have knowledge of good and evil and choose righteously to stand in solidity for all things GREAT.
My body is my friend, as I am grateful for it. We are connected and operate as one.

My body works hard to take care of me, because it is informed of its duties while I am here. I respect it for its service, as it is appreciative for its use.

In God's great name, I ask that you hear my prayer in its purity and serve me the vessel I am deserved. AMEN.

Reclaiming Yourself

I call to you, and ask that you hear my voice. Creator, ancestors, gods, good spirits, and the hidden, whom names I both know and do not, whose memories are woven through the fabric of existence. Whose bones lie beneath this land in which we have conquered and ruled.

Be my mirror and my sword. Break all manner of assaults attached to my spirit and return them to their originators, forever being returned upon them. Sever all of their toxic lingering attachments and defend me from harm and misfortune. Return the blessings my enemies attempted to steal from me. Let their own words be the poison from which they drink; let them swallow their own curses, being sweet to the taste, but sour to the stomach. I call back to my good fortunes, given to the unrighteous in my failure to see with eyes to see.
My defense I pray to be impenetrable. It shall not be twisted. It shall stand strong in truth. The truth shall not be shy.

I recall all of the blessings I have spoken over those who are now considered my enemies. Every prayer for their protection, prosperity, sound mind, of their stellar health and massive fortune, of their cleared paths, for all the works in their favor - I revoke them of my energy. I recall that energy into myself. May my own life be full of that protection, prosperity, sound mind, stellar health and massive fortunes, and of cleared paths. I recall my power from my enemies, from which they do not have permission to use and thrive upon. I recall these spiritual and energetic investments, unblemished and full of love as they ever were and still remain, and restore them into myself. I am an unmatched beacon for flourishing abundance. I breathe, speak, and know the truths that I will share with the masses because my energy has been fully restored to my soul.

May we once again walk forward in faith and true abundance, unbelievable to the masses. In God's name, AMEN.

Prayer for Success

I call to you, and ask that you hear my voice. Creator, ancestors, gods, good spirits, and the hidden, whom names I both know and do not, whose memories are woven through the fabric of existence. Whose bones lie beneath this land in which we have conquered and ruled.

I ask that every aspect of my life be enhanced, directed, and abound with success.

Leave no stone unturned and no corner untouched in finding my shortcomings so that I may correct them. My life vibrates with enrichment in every breath, knowing my fate ultimately ends in success. I am merely waiting my time for you to push me toward the next step of my awareness, so that I may utilize this for my benefit towards the adversaries to ensure my completion.
Let the Crown I wear exist as a beacon for upwardly spiraling prosperity and good

luck for both myself and others with ears to hear and eyes to see.

I pray you protect me from jealousy, envy, misfortune, and failure. Clear my path while harming none, and lead me onward into the way.

If there are obstacles, I choose overcome them. If the deck is stacked against me, I will use my experiences to guide me through. I sever myself from all vampires that do exist, they may not feed off of my energy any longer. They do not have permission to access me.

My success will not be divorced from my spirit, ever and ever. In God's name, AMEN.

- CONCLUSION -

Upon near completion of this Book number 3 I realized I had left out a very major factor within Books 1 and 2. I left out the power of Creator, The Most High. I had chosen to do my best to leave this out to not cause a stir. The simple truth of the matter is, without faith, you have not much else to go on when things are tough. With the acceptance of faith, you will find a new place of serenity and peace. Faith is the largest key I will ever be able to provide to you in truth.

Fear is separate from danger. Fear is a trap, danger is a genuine concern. Fear is to be overcome, danger is to be avoided.

Within the constructs of our reality, something brought YOU all the way from finding a bead, to here. Learn faith in truth. Not the truth you are taught, the undeniable truth. You know the truth, if you have to question it, be wary. Trust what is divinely sent, but use discretion, the evil roam freely as well. Take the leap, trust the path, and go for it. You will regret if you don't , and you have to overcome fear to experience both failure and success. Do not wait, the waiting is the trap. Yet do not rush; this prevents costly error. Listen and be guided by The Way.

YOU are to be a creator of your own reality. Do not listen to the masses about how a cookie taste, taste of it yourself. It is something that is to be experienced one on one. Not someone else directing you, quieten yourself and listen. You hold within you the greatest keys to ever be found. It is waiting and ready for you to listen. TAP IN, it will guide you, if you listen.

As you utilize these Dzi beads, know that you are focusing your subconscious on a goal. A fixed intent that you seek. Allow your inner being to lead you from here to there.

I ask that you take one single solitary moment to appreciate the knowledge that has been allowed to you, the most expensive magical item that ever was, now a part of you and your journey. It has been my ultimate pleasure to share my knowledge with you.

Sincerely,

Tilii Bolin

www.ingramcontent.com/pod-product-compliance
Lightning Source LLC
Chambersburg PA
CBHW070345270326
41926CB00017B/4001